CONTENTS

YOUR GUIDE TO ANCIENT ROME

The story of Rome has gripped the world for thousands of years. How did this small village became the world's biggest city, at the heart of a mighty empire? The editors of *HAIL!* reveal the stories that made our pages from 2,300 to 1,500 years ago. You, the reader, can judge just why we shall never forget the great days of Ancient Rome.

LOOKING BACK

When did the Roman age begin, and how has the way we live changed over the centuries? The *HAIL!* review starts here...

753 BCE THE FOUNDING OF ROME

According to legend, this was the date that Rome was founded. Its first king was said to be Romulus who, with his twin Remus, had been raised by a she-wolf. His father was Mars, the god of war. In 509 BCE, the Romans threw out their kings and created a republic. By the third century BCE, the Roman republic controlled all of Italy.

27 BCE ROME BECOMES AN EMPIRE

From this time onwards, Rome was ruled by emperors. The empire was at its greatest in 117 CE, covering a large area of Europe, Asia and North Africa. In the fifth century CE, power shifted away from the city of Rome to a new capital in the east called Constantinople.

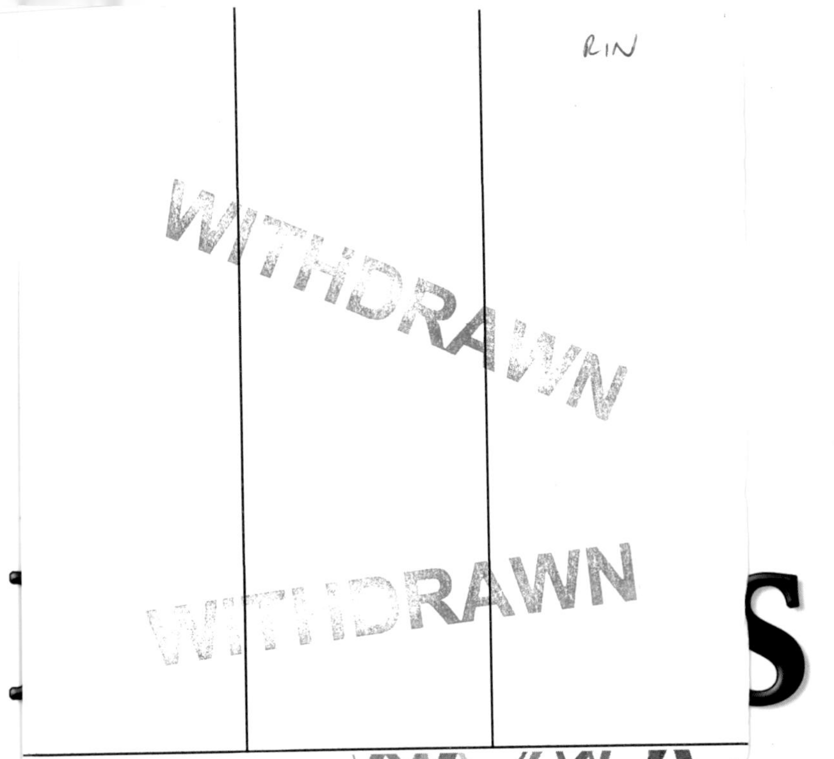

Philip Steele

WAYLAND

WAYLAND

This edition published in 2013 by Wayland

Wayland
Hachette Children's Books
338 Euston Road
London NW1 3BH

Wayland Australia
Level 17/207 Kent Street
Sydney, NSW 2000

Brown Bear Books Ltd.
First Floor
9–17 St. Albans Place
London
N1 0NX

Author: Philip Steele
Managing editor: Miranda Smith
Designer: Lorna Phillips
Picture researcher: Clare Newman
Design manager: David Poole
Editorial director: Lindsey Lowe
Children's publisher: Anne O'Daly
Consultant: Dr Paul G. Bahn

British Library Cataloguing in Publication Data

Steele, Philip, 1948-
Ancient Romans. — (Hail!)
1. Rome—History—Empire 30 B.C.–476 A.D.—Juvenile literature.
2. Rome—Civilization—Juvenile literature.
I. Title II. Series
937'.06-dc23

ISBN-13: 978 0 7502 7172 1

Printed in China

Wayland is a division of Hachette Children's Books, an Hachette UK company.
www.hachette.co.uk

Websites

The website addresses (URLs) included in this book were valid at the time of going to press. However, because of the nature of the internet, it is possible that some addresses may have changed, or sites may have changed or closed down since publication. While the author and publisher regret any inconvenience this may cause the readers, no responsibility for any such changes can be accepted by either the author or the publisher.

PICTURE ACKNOWLEDGEMENTS

Key: b = bottom, bgr = background, c = centre, is = insert , l = left, mtg = montage, r = right, t = top.

Front Cover: Art Archive: Gianni Dagli Orti tc; iStockphoto: David Luscombe br; Shutterstock: James Steidl l Thinkstock: tr.
Interior: Alamy: Ivy Oak Images 10br, Universal Images Group Limited 11bc; Art Archive: Gianni Dagli Orti 7br; Bridgeman Art Library: 9tr; Corbis: Alinari Archives 27br, Araldo De Luca 20cl, 20cr, Stapleton Collection 23tl, Werner Forman 25tr; iStockphoto: Danila Ascione 14cl, Angelina Dimitrova 17cl, Foto Voyager 7bl, Hedda Gjerpen 7t, Mikhail Khromar 26br, David Luscombe 9bl, Bart Parren 21cl, Marisa Allegra Williams 14bl; Jupiter Images: 7tr; Kobal Collection: Bryna/Universal 16tr; Mary Evans Picture Library: 5br, 17tc, 19cr, 22cl; Photolibrary: Adam Woolfitt/Robert Harding Travel 28cr; Shutterstock: 3drenderings 11bl, Algol 19cl, Ayazad 29tc, Thomas Barrat 24clm, Benedictus 14cr, Katrina Brown 10tc, 12tc, Bryan Busoicki 20/21 bgr, Margo Harrison 6l, 7rl, J. Helgason 22/23b, 28b, Eric Isselee 12tr, 24bl, Jaba 13cb, Etien Jones 26/27, Oleksandr Koral 21cr, Vladimir Korostyshevskiy 28bc, Max Stock Photo 30/31, Mointain Pix 21br, N.N. 22t, Tyler Olson 20br, Regien Paassen 11br, K. Pavel 4cl, 15tl, Denis Pepin 8crb, Myron Pronyshyn 27tr, Pseudolongino 16br, Pshenichka 6tr, Laurent Renault 8/9 bgr, Rolandino 12bl, David H. Seymour 25bl, James Steidl 13ct, Ian Stewart 15br, Andrey Solomin 28tr, SV Lumagraphica 19bc, Irena Tischenko 18tl, Tomashko 18tr, 18bc, David Turner 11cl, Sergey Vasilyev 27cl, Vibrant Image Studio 14/15 bgr, Pippa West 5bl 6/7, Edd Westmancott 18bl, Witchcraft 15tr, Av.d Wolde 3br, 29br; Thinkstock: 13cr, 15cr, 16bl, 17cr, 26cl; Topham: 5bc, 13t, Roger-Viollet 8crt, 26bl, The Ganger Collection 8cl, 17bl, 19tl. 21b, 23br, 24cr, 29cr, The Museum of London/HIP 13br.

HAIL! QUIZ WHY IS ROME A SUPERPOWER?

Enter our readers' poll and select your favourite from these five key achievements:

1. WAR AND PEACE
Rome is the most formidable military power the world has ever seen. Our legions are professional and highly trained, and are led by many brilliant generals. Our armies have brought peace and prosperity to the empire.

2. ENTERPRISE AND BUSINESS
Our ships bring wheat from Africa, marble from Greece and wool from Britain. Thriving industries such as wine production and pottery have extended to Gaul and Germany. Across the empire there is taxation and a single currency. And we import luxury goods and spices from distant lands in Asia.

3. ENGINEERING AND TECHNOLOGY
Romans have literally been building the Europe of the future. New cities are linked by a network of finely engineered roads, the most advanced the world has ever seen. Our soaring aqueducts carry water supplies, and we have invented concrete, that marvel of the modern age.

4. THE ARTS
The Latin language is spoken across the empire and is used by writers, poets, historians and philosophers. There are open-air theatres in every city. We enjoy music, and decorate our homes with wall paintings and mosaics, and our cities with monuments and statues.

5. LAW AND ORDER
Romans enjoy the rule of law and have law courts in all our cities. Our punishments are often very harsh, and our lawyers are often too rich, but the system works. Our laws will influence the world for thousands of years.

Submit Your Answer

SEE INSIDE:

I ♥ Rome pp. 6–7

Circus Maximus pp. 7, 13

Cleopatra p.22

REGULAR CONTRIBUTORS: Decimus the Gladiator, Julia Augusta Agrippina, Trajan

I ♥ ROME

Your guide to the big fig!

There is nowhere else like it in the world – the buzz, the action, the energy! No wonder all our (long and very straight) roads lead to Rome. It is the hub of the universe and has been for hundreds of years. It was not built in a day, you know. *HAIL!* can say with confidence, "Prepare to be awed!"

When to go

- ✔ In winter it is milder in Rome than in the northern parts of the empire. Join in the fun of the Saturnalia festival, 17–25 December.
- ✔ Spring has flowers in bloom on every balcony. Beware the Ides (15th) of March, when Julius Caesar was killed.
- ✔ Summer on the streets can be as hot as Vulcan's forge and smelly, too. Chill out beside tinkling fountains in shady gardens.
- ✔ Autumn? Lovely, golden days and a bit cooler, too.

Still in doubt? Ask your soothsayer for the most favourable time.

TIP FOR VISITORS

In Rome you may see many things that you find shocking or odd. Don't stop and stare, and never start an argument or a fight! When in Rome, do as the Romans do ...

HAIL! SAYS HAIL!

Q Ave! I believe you have just arrived in Ostia, the port of Rome?

A Yes, my name is Marcus Didius Valens and I've just sailed here from Gades (modern Cadiz) in south-western Spain.

Q And what are your first impressions of our wonderful city?

A The River Tiber stinks, the merchants rip you off and the bars are noisy and full of drunken slave traders, sailors and soldiers.

Q Well I assure you when you reach the city walls you will be amazed!

A Let's hope so. This little trip has cost me a good few denarii!

THE ETERNAL CITY

Hello, my name is Apollonia and I am your guide for today. I am wearing a purple *stola* so you can pick me out easily in the crowds. We shall be visiting some of the most amazing sites in the world, and you will be impressed, believe me!

JUST FOLLOW THE GUIDE!

◄ COLOSSEUM

The massive Colosseum can hold 50,000 spectators. Today, we will be able to watch the parade of the gladiators and, if there is time, see some bloody combat in the arena.

▲ ROMAN FORUM

We shall be visiting the Roman Forum, the heart of this city and the empire. There you can see the statues and temples, as well as the whizz-kid traders and politicians at work.

▲ TRAJAN'S COLUMN

Trajan's Column is a marvel at 38 metres (125 ft) high. It is covered with carved pictures of our brave legions fighting in Dacia.

▼ CIRCUS MAXIMUS

You have the option of a visit to the Circus Maximus, the chariot racing track, which can pack in 250,000 fans. The daring and skill of the charioteers is unforgettable.

▲ AQUEDUCTS

Some 750 million litres of water a day flow into Rome through these water channels. Many people spend half the day at the public baths so the city needs lots of water.

BEWARE!

Traffic jams, even by night...crowds...noise... Well, there are nearly a million people living in this city!

▲ DRAINS AND SEWERS

The Cloaca Maxima is the mega-sewer of the world. Did you know that we Romans have a goddess of sewage, called Cloacina?

FRIENDS, ROMANS, COUNTRYMEN...

We are all Romans, but we come in all shapes and sizes, as well as classes. So, just who are we and what makes us tick? In this special survey, *HAIL!* decided to interview all sorts of people around the city, and then invite our readers to comment on what they had to say.

SLAVES — WHERE WOULD WE BE WITHOUT THEM?

"My slave name is Decimus. I was captured as a prisoner-of-war ten years ago and sold in a slave auction at Ostia. There were all sorts for sale that day — Greeks, Gauls, Germanics, Britons, Africans, Thracians...men, women and children. Now I work in my master's townhouse, fetching and carrying all day long."

YOU WRITE:

Well, this Decimus does sound a bit sorry for himself! The gods deal us all a cruel blow from time to time, and there's nothing we can do about that, so don't blame us.
CENSORIUS, CAPUA

LET'S HEAR IT FOR THE PLEBEIANS!

"*Ave!* My name is Caius Oppius Felix and I am a butcher. My knives and cleavers are as sharp as a gladiator's sword. My wife Licinia prepares the pies and sausages, and does the accounts. It's we Plebeians — the ones who don't come from noble families — who have made Rome what it is today."

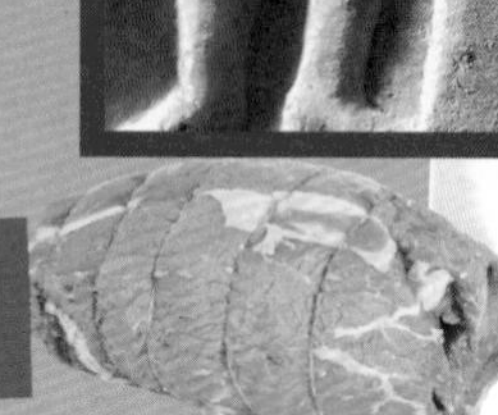

YOU WRITE:

I absolutely agree! CORNELIA, FLORENTIA

In the days of the old republic, we Plebs had to fight for our rights. We even had our own Plebeian Council. Now we're ruled by emperors, we don't hear so much about our rights any more.
PUBLIUS, MISENUM

A CLASS ACT OR POSH TOSH?

" Good evening and welcome to my lovely home. We also have a beautiful villa in Campania (see pp.14–15) and our household has the services of about 400 slaves. I just love planning banquets and parties. Well now, my name is Claudia Sabina. My husband, of course, is a senator with many business and political interests. I myself am related to the imperial family, so we are especially fortunate. Did you know my line of ancestry goes back almost to Romulus himself! We are the cream of the Patricians, my dear, so only the very best match will do for my sons and daughters when it comes to marriage. "

YOU WRITE:

We all know how her husband is a crook. And why is her daughter always sighing over the gladiators at the barracks if she is so classy? FLAVIA, POMPEII

Her husband sponsors some of the best games at the amphitheatre, so that family will always get my vote. AELIUS, POMPEII

If I had known you were going to put me on the same page as slaves and butchers, I would never have agreed to this interview! CLAUDIA SABINA, ROMA

DAGGERS DRAWN

"*Keep us happy – or else!*"

" At your service, Postumus Didius Galba, of the Praetorian Guard. We are bodyguards to the most powerful man in the world, the emperor of Rome, but these days it is we who are the most powerful people of all. If the emperor crosses us, we can always arrange a little accident! That's politics, Praetorian style. We are paid to keep our ears and eyes open, and we often get a little bonus to keep quiet. "

YOU WRITE:

If you ask me, the stench of corruption in Rome today is worse than the Cloaca Maxima. TERTIUS, ROMA

It always was! GNAEUS, ROMA

What an attractive bunch! Those guys look so smart, standing guard in their fancy armour and crests! ANTONIA, BONONIA

FIGHTING FIT!

From the deserts of North Africa to the cities of Asia, from the Rhine frontier to the River Danube, our troops are keeping the barbarians at bay. But what is it really like to serve in distant parts of the empire? *HAIL!* has sent its reporters to the front line, to see how our lads are faring.

Q What are you wearing and carrying?

A My helmet and armour, strong leather shoes, a spear, a dagger, my shield, a bed roll and pots and pans.

Q So why have you got a shovel in your kit?

A When we make camp we dig ourselves in, just in case of attack. That's our leather tent on the mule.

Q Expecting trouble, then?

A We are. But I've got the very latest segmented armour and my deadly short sword, my *gladius*.

> *"... and we always win."*

Q Does the legion give you decent food?

A Hard-baked biscuits, a bit of fatty bacon or rancid cheese, washed down with sour wine.

GET YOUR WEAPONS HERE

- ***gladius:*** various styles of short swords
- ***pilum:*** the finest throwing spears in Rome
- ***pugio:*** those essential sidearm daggers
- ***scutum:*** shields with designs to order
- ***sudarium focale, cingulum*** and ***tunica:*** scarf, belt and tunic of the finest materials
- ***caligae:*** military boots of strong leather

HURRY! SALE ENDS SOON!

HADRIAN'S WALL!

Our reporter Tertius Manlius Capito is embedded with the First Tungrian Cohort at Vercovicium (Housesteads) on Hadrian's Wall, in remote Britannia.

The weather is as miserable as Hades here on the northern edge of the empire. It either rains, sleets or snows. It has taken decades for Rome to round up the Brit rebels. Now, thanks to emperor Hadrian, Romans can sleep peacefully at night. A new wall crosses the north to keep out the Caledonian hordes.

Where have all our soldiers gone? They're settling down all over the empire when they retire!

Dear Sister,
My time out here in Egypt is over. I've served Rome well these last 20 years, but now it is time to hang up my shield and collect my pension. I've decided to stay out here and marry my girlfriend, who is from Alexandria. I am setting up in business selling Egyptian cloth. When I am a rich man I shall send you enough money to make the voyage here from Ostia.

Give my love to your little ones.

Draco

WEAPONS OF MASS DESTRUCTION

These are some of the empire's most persuasive ambassadors!

1

The Ballista A heavy-duty catapult firing round stone shot. Ideal for siege warfare.

2

The Onager Kicks like a mule and hurls massive boulders or flaming missiles at a city's walls.

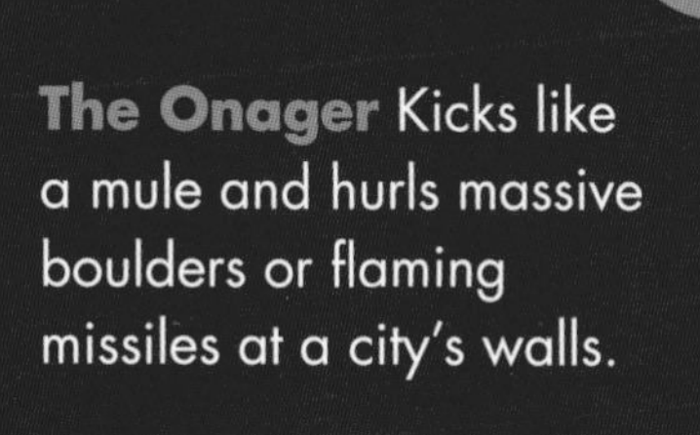

3

The Testudo (the tortoise) This strong, tight formation protects soldiers, allowing units to march right up to enemy fortifications.

No need to miss out — Rome has taken its talents to the far reaches of the world. All over the Roman empire there are wonderful plays being staged, chariot-races being run and gladiatorial fights to the death. Just watch these pages for *HAIL!*'s recommendations and comments.

THEATRE LISTINGS

POMPEII AT THE SMALL THEATRE

Coming soon: A new comedy by Plautus.
A hilarious tale of mix-ups and misunderstandings.
Not to be missed, especially the Prologue!

"I LAUGHED OUT LOUD!" *What's On in Campania*

ARAUSIO THEATRE, GAUL

Now showing: Seneca's *Phaedra*,
a tragic story from ancient Greece.

"A SHOCKER! NICE MASKS, THOUGH..." *South Gaul Echo*

JUST DYING TO GIVE US A GOOD TIME!

***HAIL!* visits the barracks to interview the man everyone is talking about — Auctus the Gladiator.**

Q *It's the big Colosseum fight tomorrow, Auctus. Are you confident?*

A Only the gods know what will happen. A gladiator who is too confident is the first to be dragged out of the arena with his throat gashed open. I'm in good condition, well fed and ready to fight for my life.

Q *Now, you will be fighting as a* Secutor. *Just what does that involve?*

A I am armed with a short sword and a shield, and matched against a *Retiarius* — that's the guy with the net and trident. I must be fast and nimble but totally ruthless.

Q *And, if you are still alive this time tomorrow?*

A Well, that would be thirty victories in a row. I am hoping to win my freedom and quit the arena for good. With my prize money I can make a new start.

Editor's note: Unfortunately, luck ran out for Auctus this time. He battled magnificently but lost the fight — and his life.

CITHARA
LESSONS OFFERED BY GREEK MUSICIAN

The ideal accomplishment for young Roman ladies

REASONABLE RATES

Contact Aphrodite
at the House by Fortune Fountain, Herculaneum

Cithara

BLUES TAKE THE BIG ONE

FATAL CRASH MARS LAP TWO

Here at the Circus Maximus it's fine and sunny with a fresh breeze – the gods are smiling on us. The rope has dropped and the four quadrigae are off! Draco is in the lead as the bronze dolphin on the central wall is dipped to mark the first of seven laps. And OH! we have a nasty collision there – Romeo won't survive those head injuries. The hooves are flying! Come on you Blues! He's there, it's Draco – another fantastic win for this young man who was a slave only a couple of years ago!

UPDATE

BUCKETS OF BLOOD

We asked spectators pouring out of the Colosseum what they had enjoyed during the day's show.

" I liked it when the women fought the dwarfs. Whoever thought that one up? Oh, and the tigers were good, too, when they leapt out from behind that rock."

"I actually saw the emperor with my own eyes! I came all the way from Brundisium to catch a glimpse."

"I felt sorry for that Auctus. He deserved to win."

"I felt a bit sick, to tell you the truth. It wasn't all that blood or the heat. I think it was the pie I ate."

GAMBLING HAS BEEN BANNED — AGAIN!

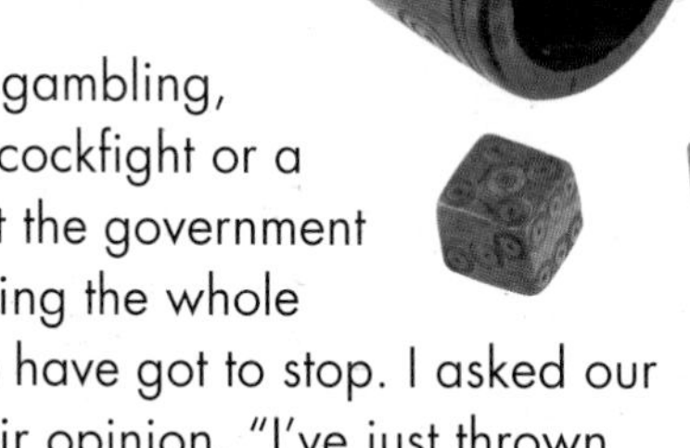

We Romans love gambling, whether it's on a cockfight or a game of dice. But the government says that it is ruining the whole economy and we have got to stop. I asked our office staff for their opinion. "I've just thrown a double six and won as much as I can earn in a whole week", explained one water-carrier.

Region of the week... CAMPANIA

For us Romans, about half the days of the year are holy days or public holidays. And what do people do with their free time? They dust off their travelling books and go and see the world! This year, why not visit the seaside in the region of Campania, southern Italy, only four days journey south of Rome.

HERCULANEUM

Just south of Neapolis, visit the pretty port of Herculaneum where you will find fresh fish, every modern convenience, fine public baths, etc. The local gods are strongman Hercules for protection, Apollo for the Sun and Venus for love – what a holiday trio!

NEAPOLIS (NAPLES)

South of Rome, this wonderful bay offers probably the most beautiful views in the whole world!

CAPRI

The latest holiday destination for the in-crowd is the lush and exclusive island of Capri, with its hidden coves (left). Caesar Augustus was the first to discover its charms. He acquired it in return for the nearby island of Ischia, which he gave to the city of Neapolis.

Did you know?

The emperor Tiberius has no fewer than 12 villas on the island of Capri, and uses the magical sea cave, the Blue Grotto, as his personal swimming pool!

POMPEII

A short ride from Herculaneum, you can visit Pompeii, under the charming slopes of Mt. Vesuvius. This is a fun city — two theatres, an amphitheatre, fantastic baths and restaurants...

AROUND THE BAY

You can stay in one of the wonderful villas in the sunny resorts lining the coastal route south of Neapolis. From nearly every viewpoint, you are able to see Mt. Vesuvius rising up majestically.

STOP PRESS 24 August 79 CE

CANCEL RESERVATIONS FOR CAMPANIA!!!

Reports have come in from all across the Campania region that volcanic Mt. Vesuvius has blown its top! Suffocating smoke is belching out of the mountain. It is raining stones over Pompeii. Herculaneum is filled with boiling mud. Thousands are reported as dead or missing, including the great writer and scientist Pliny the Elder! Poor old chap. Is this the end of tourism in Campania?

NOTE: ALL BOAT TRIPS CANCELLED AND ROADS CLOSED UNTIL FURTHER NOTICE.

HOW ABOUT THE SEVEN WONDERS TOUR INSTEAD?

Don't leave graffiti on the ancient monuments!

See the world's top seven wonders, as listed by Antipater of Sidon

1 The GREAT PYRAMID in Egypt. The tallest monument in the world.

2 The PHAROS at Alexandria. The world's biggest lighthouse.

3 The STATUE OF ZEUS AT OLYMPIA, GREECE (we Romans call him Jove or Jupiter).

4 The COLOSSUS OF RHODES This tumbled down in an earthquake, but it's still impressive.

5 The MAUSOLEUM at Halicarnassus. This is the ultimate royal tomb.

6 The TEMPLE AT EPHESUS. Make a pilgrimage to honour the goddess Diana.

7 BABYLON's hanging gardens — but there is fighting in Mesopotamia at the moment.

CELEBRITIES

We Romans invented them!

Here at *HAIL!* we have been going through our archives. The names of the greatest and most famous Romans will live forever but we have to admit that, over the centuries, there have been some rather bad apples as well.

REBEL ROUSER

Spartacus (c.109–71 BCE) was Rome's "most wanted" rebel. This tough guy from Thrace was an ex-soldier, ex-slave and ex-gladiator. He was also a one-time star of the arena – until he started a slave rebellion that became a full-scale war against the government. He was a bit of a hunk, and some of us did rather admire his gutsiness... but he can hardly have been surprised when he and 6,600 supporters found themselves crucified along the Appian Way.

DID YOU KNOW?
The Appian Way is a road leading from Rome to south-east Italy.

EMPIRE BUILDER

We once knew him simply as Octavius (63 BCE–14 CE), and he was the great-nephew and adopted son of Julius Caesar. Then he became **Imperator (Emperor) Caesar Augustus**. The old republicans would be turning in their graves. Augustus appointed himself to every important government job. However, the Roman world was pretty peaceful under his rule and it certainly got a lot bigger.

VENI, VIDI, VICI

In Latin, that means "I came, I saw, I conquered". And **Julius Caesar** (100–44 BCE) did just that, bringing Gaul under Roman control and invading Britain. He was a cunning politician, but did fame go to his head? He did win far too much personal power and made too many enemies. His assassination set off a civil war and marked the end of Rome as a republic.

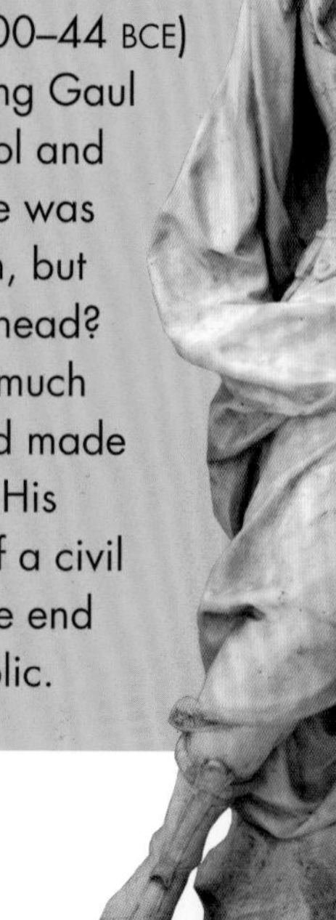

Pretty Dangerous

Julia Augusta Agrippina (15–59 CE)
What a good-looking woman! She is the great-granddaughter of one emperor, the great-niece of another, the sister of another, the wife of another and the mother of a fifth. The word is "well-connected". Other words we might use to describe her are "efficient", "ambitious" and "charming". A history maker.

Ed's note: Now that dear Agrippina the Younger is no longer with us, we can be a bit more honest. She was "ruthless, big-headed, violent and dangerous". She probably poisoned her husband, the emperor Claudius, and her son Nero tried to kill her time and again.

TWO OF THE GOOD GUYS

Trajan (53–117 CE, left) was the first Spanish-born emperor. He was a superb soldier, conquering Dacia and bringing back piles of gold and many slaves. After the Dacian Wars, his triumph or celebration lasted 123 days! Trajan rebuilt many parts of Rome, making it the fabulous city it is today. Trajan's adopted son **Hadrian** (76–138 CE, right), became the next emperor. Hadrian was very brainy for an emperor, and he ruled well. He is possibly best known for Hadrian's Wall in the north of England.

THE CIRCUS GIRL

The last person to feature in the *HAIL!* archives ended up as a Christian saint. **Theodora** (500–548 CE) is the toast of the capital of our eastern empire, called Constantinople, or Byzantium. In her day, Theodora has been many things — a circus star, an actress, a traveller and an entertainer. She is now the wife of our great emperor Justinian, and she is also a powerful ruler in her own right.

GOOD FOOD GUIDE

Romans like nothing better than a good meal and we put together wonderful feasts, with the best ingredients and entertainment. The most well-travelled Roman has found nothing better elsewhere in the world. Our delicacies include fish pickle, roasted meats, minced dormice, cakes stuffed with live thrushes and honeyed wines.

CHEF OF THE YEAR!

They say that cooking is the new gladiatorial combat. Certainly the publishing sensation of this year is a ... COOK BOOK. Its unknown author goes by the name of Apicius, and the title is *De Re Coquinaria* (*On the Subject of Cooking*). So what does chef recommend today? Take your pick from his amazing three-star menu.

Rose hips with calf's brain custard

❖

Poached eels in plum sauce

❖

Artichoke dressed with fish pickle

❖

Hot braised goose with cold sauce

❖

Milk-fed snails

ETIQUETTE (that means how to behave politely in company!)

- ✔ Wear bare feet to the table. The slave will wash them before you start.
- ✔ Wear a lightweight, fashionable gown called a *synthesis*.
- ✔ Wash greasy fingers in the bowl provided.
- ✔ Always mix your wine with water in polite company.
- ✔ Don't argue loudly or swear — but you may belch away to your heart's content!

A belly-busting banquet!

A feast given by the emperor Vitellius must hold the world record – 2,000 fish and 7,000 game birds gobbled down in one session, along with peacock brains and flamingo tongues! Old Vitellius never spent less than 400,000 sesterces on a feast, and often invited himself to four of them a day.

We asked Romans what they thought about that:

"A disgusting waste of money, since you ask. I hope he chokes on it."

"If we can make do with a nice bit of bacon, cabbage, olives, fruit and honey, why can't he?"

"Hmm! Sounds good to me! Feeling hungry already..."

THROWING A DINNER PARTY?

Make sure that your triclinium, or dining room, is beautifully decorated and well lit. Fine wall paintings are often a good conversation piece among guests. On a warm summer's evening, you may care to eat outdoors in the garden, amid statues and scented roses. Place any celebs on a central couch and flatter them generously. Provide napkins.

A TIP: If you want to show off your newfound wealth, feel free to provide dozens of fancy or novelty dishes, plenty of gold leaf and singing waiters.

Fast food – and make it saucy!

Too much business in the Forum? On the way to the Colosseum? Grab a takeaway on the street – a nice sausage, perhaps, kebabs seasoned with herbs or honey, or some tapas and olives, bread rolls. And make that with plenty of fish sauce please. Fish sauce goes with everything!

WANTED
TOP CHEF

TOP CHEF to supervise whole kitchen team, including pastry cooks, meat carvers, wine butlers and waiters. Latest well-equipped kitchens with wood-burning stoves, teams of slaves and water carriers.

GAIUS PETRONIUS ARBITER, ROMA

EXCLUSIVE OFFER
TO ALL READERS OF *HAIL!*

An elegant *thermospodium* is the must-have item for every lover of refreshment. Fashioned from the finest bronze, it is decorated with elegant winged figures. It includes a large cylinder heated by a charcoal burner, and a handy tap to release all that delicious mulled wine on a chilly autumn evening. Feel the warm glow! Impress your friends!

STYLE ON FILE

HOT LOOK FOR WOMEN

DRUSILLA is wearing a *stola* over an under-tunic, with her *palla* draped just so and fastened with a *fibula*. She wears gold earrings, but note that she does not overdo the jewellery. Her makeup is classic white face powder made of (poisonous) lead, blusher, lipstick made of red ochre or wine dregs and eye shadow of ash and saffron. And is that hair all her own? My guess is she is wearing a wig. And I bet it took a good few slaves to get her looking that good early in the morning!

HOT LOOK FOR MEN

MARCUS the soldier is bearded, and his body has been well oiled and scraped clean at the baths. He is dressed for ceremonial occasions. He wears a tunic and long, leather sandals, as well as a cotton cloak imported from Egypt. Very nice — but take a look at that fancy metal work on his armour. That will have set him back a fair bit of cash.

OUTLANDISH!

Yes, it's true: those silly Celtic and Asian barbarians wear trousers! Not shorts worn under tunics like our brave troops, but full-length trousers. Come on you barbarians, don't you think trousers look just a bit girly? What's wrong with a tunic?

JUST ARRIVED IN OSTIA!

Shimmering silks from China!

The best white linen from Egypt! Colourful cottons from India! Literally cool — and they look cool too! But can you afford these exotic imports? *HAIL!* says do not despair! Nothing looks as elegant as the classical look with the finest woollens from Tarentum.

GIRLS!

Are you athletic?

Are you the type that works out at the baths or performs acrobatics? If you are, then one of our new range of leather bikinis may be just the thing for you. Stay cool, move freely and keep lifting those weights!

THE BIG DAY

What to wear for your wedding

Hello girls! Over 12 years old? Then you probably have engagement and marriage on your mind. But what will you wear? Well, your mother will have the final say, of course. A long straight tunic of the finest cloth, traditional but flattering, and a fine orange veil for your head. And a knotted girdle around the waist – only your new hubby will be allowed to untie that! Gold rings will be exchanged. What about a wreath of flowers for your hair? Marjoram or fragrant verbena are traditional, but *HAIL!* can report a growing fashion for orange blossom. Or what about myrtle, which honours Venus, goddess of love?

ARE YOUNG PEOPLE'S FASHIONS GOING TO THE DOGS?

SENIOR CITIZENS MISS THE STYLES OF YESTERYEAR

Grandpa

"Today's men have no idea. In our day, we wore our togas with pride – 6 metres (20 ft) of heavy woollen cloth wrapped round the body and draped over the shoulder. Heavy and uncomfortable to be sure, but it did give a man a bit of class, a badge of his rank. Today, even Patricians may be seen wearing the most unsuitable garments."

Grandma

"When I was a girl we did our spinning and weaving of wool at home. Today's young women are too lazy by half. They just go to the shops and buy the cloth already woven and dyed."

SERIAL MURDER! PARANOIA! PSYCHODRAMA!

***HAIL!* lifts the lid on some of the biggest scandals that rocked the Roman world — and wonders if a few of our most famous sons and daughters were not missing a marble or two...**

CLEOPATRA ROLLED IN A RUG, THEN KILLED BY A SNAKE!

The Greek ruler of Egypt, Cleopatra VII, had a steamy affair with Julius Caesar. In fact, she had herself presented to him all rolled up in a Persian carpet. After Julius was murdered in 44 BCE, Cleo did not just form a political alliance with Mark Antony, she fell for him too — and in quite a big way. When, in 30 BCE, Mark Antony was finally defeated by his rival Octavian (who later became the emperor Caesar Augustus), Cleo committed suicide by snakebite. ***Ouch!***

HAIL! comments

Cleo was not a real looker, but they all fell for her. Perhaps it was the rug. Or perhaps it was her beauty treatment — they say she bathed in the milk of 700 asses (mules) every day! Cleo did have a tough time of it, but then that's politics for you. And her loss was Rome's gain, for Egypt now came under direct Roman rule.

CALIGULA TOO BIG FOR HIS "LITTLE BOOTS"

Caligula ("little boots") was the nickname of Gaius Julius Caesar Germanicus, emperor of Rome. He was born in 12 CE, the son of a successful and popular general. Caligula claimed to be a god, and killed all sorts of people. He tried to make his horse Incitatus a consul of Rome, keeping him in a marble stable and feeding him gold flakes from an ivory manger. Caligula ordered his troops to attack Britain. When they reached the coast of northern France, he sent them to collect seashells from the beach instead. He claimed they were his spoils of war. He was murdered in 41 CE.

"*My horse understands me best!*"

HAIL! comments

Everyone agrees that Caligula was cruel and crazy, but what made him that way? In 37 CE he was very ill for a time and his madness may have followed on from this sickness. Mind you, it seems to have been rather difficult for anyone to be emperor at that time and stay sane!

NERO, NERO, NOBODY'S HERO

Nero ruled Rome from 54 to 68 CE. He had his mother executed and many more deaths followed. In 64 CE there was a big fire in Rome during which, it is said, Nero sang on stage. He blamed the fire on a new religious sect called the Christians. As punishment, he ordered them torn apart by dogs, crucified or burnt alive. In 67 CE Nero entered the Olympic Games as a charioteer and nearly killed himself. The following year he commited suicide to avoid execution.

HAIL! comments

The funny thing was that Nero was popular with ordinary people in Rome. Could it be that some of the bad things he is said to have done were exaggerated by his enemies? Our guess is that he really did deserve his reputation as one of the worst emperors ever!

THE COUNTRY LIFESTYLE

IS IT FOR YOU?

LOCATION is everything when it comes to building your own little palace in the countryside, says *HAIL!*'s property correspondent.

DON'T...

- ✗ build your villa on the slopes of a volcano such as Vesuvius, however fertile the soil. A lot of people did – and a lot of people died in the eruption of 79 CE
- ✗ build your villa in a war zone, or where the natives are likely to burn it down or poison your well during a revolt
- ✗ choose such a nice site that some jealous emperor takes a fancy to it and demands it as a gift

DO...

- ✓ build near good woodland where you can spend the day hunting
- ✓ build on fertile farmland that will turn in a tidy profit
- ✓ ensure there is a clean water supply
- ✓ make sure there is enough civilised company in the neighbourhood to provide you with dinner guests
- ✓ make sure that there is a good messenger service to the nearest city, to keep in touch with news from Rome

Bored? GO HUNTING!

Set up a hunting party and be a hero of the chase. Bring home a wild boar from the forest (you can dine out on that story for years). And if you do not spear a boar, you can enjoy a picnic.

Thank your lucky stars

You are successful and wealthy, but you are as nothing if you forget one thing — a *lararium*, or shrine to the household gods. If you want your new villa to prosper, make a small offering of wine or food at their shrine every day, and say a prayer.

It's yours if the price is right

Let me take you round this select villa property. You will see that the land has been well cared for and yields really first-rate harvests. There is a delightful dovecote and the ponds are stocked with the tastiest fish. Nearer the house, we can see an established herb garden with fine statues and tall cypress trees. Just look at those fantastic views across the River Padus.

Entering the villa, there are two *atria*, and these open into the fine bedrooms. In this large room on the left, the master receives guests and there is an estate office. There is a summer dining room as well as a winter one.

Over here is a superb bath house. You may be a long way from Rome, but you can still luxuriate in a hot tub for as long as the slaves keep the furnace burning.

Furnaces keep the underfloor heating going in winter. The warm air flows and even heats the flues in the wall.

Do you admire these mosaics? Beautiful, aren't they? A really lively geometric design runs across the floor. And on the walls, these paintings look so real! The blue and orange are very much this year's colours in Rome.

A villa costs a fortune, but good management will pay it back over the years. Remember, the estates produce fruit, grain, wool, honey and wine or olives. Wherever you settle in the empire, the produce will make you richer! No labour costs (thanks to slaves), lucrative contracts and all the wine you can drink.

OLD RELIGIONS,

Our ancient temples are our pride and glory across the empire. We have many gods, and they each have a different area of our lives that they watch over. But more and more people are turning to eastern cults. *HAIL!* charts how attitudes towards faith and belief have changed over the years.

PIETY PAYS, BY JOVE!

We sacrifice animals to the gods that made Rome great. We pour out our best wine as offerings. All these rituals keep the gods happy and on the side of us puny mortals. On these pages are just a few of the gods you need to keep on your side.

JUNO

Getting married? Want to have a baby? Juno's the goddess for you...

MARS

Are you a politician who fancies starting a war, or a general off to invade a distant land? Don't forget to make a sacrifice to Mars, god of war. He will be very angry if you do not. Surely you have noticed that the planet Mars is red, the colour of blood?

JUPITER OR JOVE

The big daddy of the gods sponsors the city of Rome. If you want to guarantee an agreement, make sure everyone swears an oath in his name. If they break their word, they will be struck by a thunderbolt.

NEW CULTS

GOOD FOR BUSINESS!

Do you want to be successful in your job? If you are a merchant, Mercury (below) will sort out your deals. If you own a vineyard, Saturn will keep the soil fertile. If you grow wheat or other cereal crops, honour the goddess Ceres.

SATURNALIA!

IT'S A TOPSY-TURVY WORLD...
Winter may be a miserable and dark time of the year, but 17–23 December is lit up by the festival of the god Saturn. What a great holiday! Saturnalia is the one time of the year we can let our hair down. Masters wait on slaves, there are presents and special feasts, candles, riotous parties, wear-what-you-like-days and legal gambling. But is it all getting out of hand? Some Romans complain that all this has precious little to do with the worship of Saturn. Do they have a point, or are they all moaning Minervas? We carried out a poll of our readers, and there was one message that came out loud and clear: Get partying!

OH! THOSE CHRISTIANS...

How times change. When Romans put a troublesome preacher called Jesus to death in Jerusalem, little did we know that people would start to worship him as the Son of God, even here in Rome. Nero put Christians to death in the arena, and Diocletian had no time for them at all. Now it seems that the emperor Constantine has had a vision and become a Christian. Who knows, perhaps Rome will one day be as famous for its churches as its temples! It seems unlikely, but you never know...

CULTS, CULTS, CULTS...

More and more Romans are turning to weird religions. The Egyptian mother goddess Isis (right) is very popular in Rome. Also, our soldiers put on funny hats and worship Mithras in secret ceremonies. Some say that cult began in Persia, some in Greece and others in Rome itself.

NEWS
LATEST

IS ROME IN DANGER?

Some people are saying our empire is in danger, as Germanic warriors break through our northern borders. We are even moving troops out of Britain to plug the gaps. Everywhere the empire seems to be going to the dogs. Is our luck running out at last? Here at *HAIL!* we say no way! Past issues reveal other crises that Romans have overcome during our long history.

GAULS!

Do you remember when the Gauls attacked Rome, back in 387 BCE? The geese on the Capitoline hill made such a racket that the invaders' cover was blown and the city was saved. Then Julius Caesar invaded Gaul and in 46 BC the Gaulish rebel chief Vercingetorix (right) was paraded through the streets of Rome in chains.

BOUDICCA!

Back in 60 CE, our readers were dismayed by reports of the Britons rising up against us under their queen, a flame-haired fury called Boudicca. She wiped out the town of Colchester and burned down London and St Albans. But Romans soon sorted her out – and now the little Brits are complaining because we are leaving!

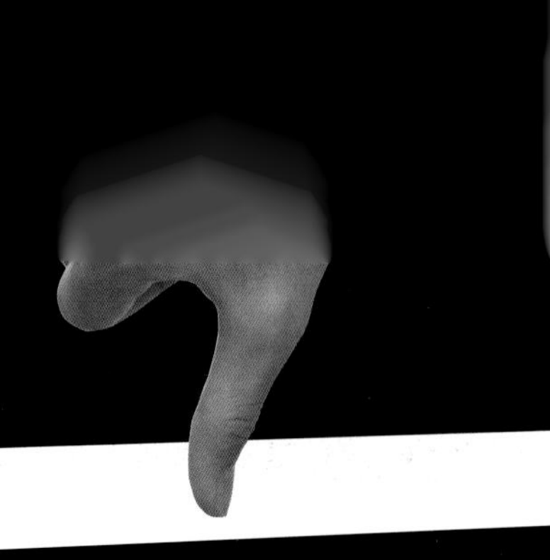

CARTHAGE!

Will we ever forget our great rivals the Carthaginians? They were based in North Africa, but in 218 BCE their general Hannibal marched the long way round — through Spain and Gaul, crossing the snowy Alps with his war elephants — to have a go at us in Italy. And what happened to Carthage? We trashed the city in 146 BCE.

ARMINIUS!

Those German tribes have always given us a hard time. In 9 CE, their chief Arminius took out three whole Roman legions in a big battle in the forest. Later he was killed by his own men. Four hundred years later, another Germanic army, the Western Goths, are heading in our direction. We'll see how they get on.

...STOP PRESS August 410 CE...

ROME SACKED BY GOTHS!!!

The gates of Rome have been opened to the enemy by our own slaves. Alaric the Goth has entered the city of Rome and for three days his men have looted all the gold and treasure they can lay their hands on. Is this the beginning of the end?

EDITORIAL NOTE

The Goths moved on, but all sorts of other Germanic tribes and kings set up in Italy during the following century. The old Roman tradition continued in the east at the city of Constantinople (Byzantium, modern Istanbul). This became the centre of a new eastern empire, one that would last for another 1,000 years.

GLOSSARY

ancestry The people in your family from whom you are descended.

aqueduct A channel or pipe used to carry water supplies, often supported by a bridge.

atrium (plural **atria**) A central court in a Roman house, with an opening in the roof.

barbarian A foreigner, someone whom the Greeks and Romans believed to be uncivilised.

barracks Buildings that house soldiers or gladiators.

Caledonians Members of various tribes occupying what is now Scotland, at the time of the Roman conquest and occupation of Britain.

civil war A war fought between groups of people from the same country.

crucify To put someone to death by nailing them or tying them to a large wooden cross.

fibula A brooch used to fasten a garment, such as a cloak.

Gaul An area that once included northern Italy, France and Belgium.

gladiator A professional fighter or slave, trained to fight to the death in the arena as public entertainment.

Goth One of various Germanic peoples who attacked and invaded parts of the Roman Empire.

Ides of March 15 March in the Roman calendar, a religious festival.

legion A large unit of the Roman army, numbering between 4,200 and 5,200 soldiers.

mausoleum A grand monumental tomb.

mosaic A picture on a wall, floor or ceiling, made up from small fragments of coloured pottery, stone or glass.

patrician A member of one of Rome's noble families who had great political power.

rancid Stale and sour, tasting unpleasant.

republic A state governed by its citizens rather than by a king, queen or emperor.

Saturnalia A midwinter festival and holiday in honour of the god Saturn.

sect A group sharing strong religious beliefs.

senator A member of the Senate, the council of state in ancient Rome.

stola A long gown worn by women.

Vulcan God of fire, often shown as a blacksmith.

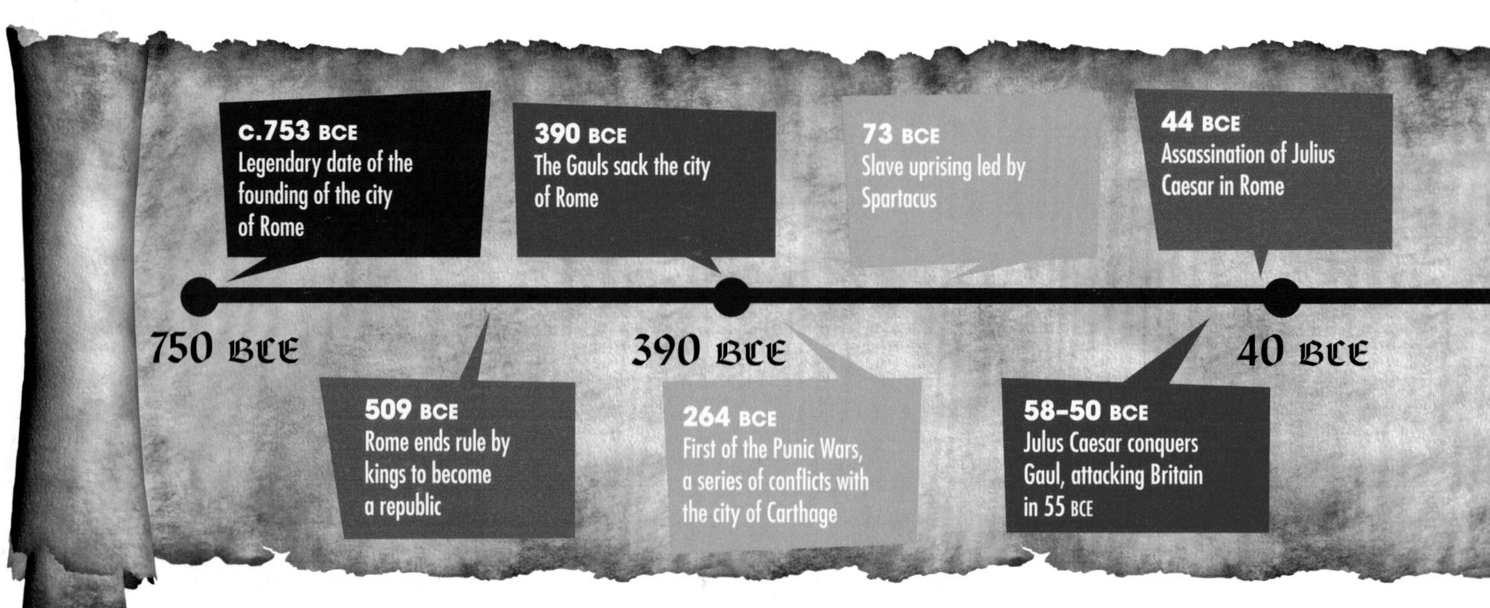

ON THE WEB

www.bbc.co.uk/history/ancient/romans/ Detailed articles on aspects of everyday life in Roman Britain and the empire as well as stimulating games.

www.channel4.com/history/microsites/H/history/guide03/ A time traveller's guide to the Roman Empire.

http://library.thinkquest.org/26602/home.htm A forum about the forum, also the army, the home, government, the arts and other topics.

www.historylink101.com/ancient_rome/ancient_rome_daily_life.htm Offers links to sites about Roman recipes, legions, sports, games and social customs.

www.exovedate.com/ancient_timeline_one.html A timeline with extended explanations and links.

http://gwydir.demon.co.uk/jo/roman/index.htm Simple but useful reference guide to the gods and goddesses of ancient Rome.

www.historylearningsite.co.uk/a_history_of_ancient_rome.htm All sorts of angles on Ancient Rome, from roads to medicine and public baths.

BOOKS

Navigators: Ancient Rome by Philip Steele (Kingfisher, 2009)

Men, Women and Children in Ancient Rome (Wayland, 2010) and ***in Roman Britain*** (Wayland, 2011) by Jane Bingham

Eyewitness: Ancient Rome by Simon James (Dorling Kindersley, 2008)

The Gruesome Truth About the Romans by Jillian Powell (Wayland, 2010)

National Geographic Investigates: Ancient Rome by Zilah Decker (National Geographic, 2007)

What Did the Ancient Romans Do For Me? by Patrick Catel (Heinemann Library, 2011)

27 BCE
Octavian starts his rule as Augustus, Rome's first emperor

79 CE
Eruption of Vesuvius destroys Pompeii and Herculaneum

476 CE
Power passes to Constantinople and the eastern empire

30 BCE — 300 CE — 500 CE

43 CE
Start of the Roman conquest of Britain

117 CE
The Roman Empire reaches its largest extent

410 CE
Western Goths sack the city of Rome

INDEX